John N. Morris

The Life Beside This One

ATHENEUM NEW YORK

1975

Certain of these poems first appeared in print as follows:

THE CHOWDER REVIEW, *Saving the Daylight*

COLLEGE ENGLISH, *Summer School*

THE DENVER QUARTERLY, *Crusoe Continuing, Not Gardening,* and *Looking For It*

HUDSON REVIEW, *Near the Potomac, Running It Backward*

THE NEW REPUBLIC, *For My Mother in the Woods, House Holding*

THE NEW YORKER, *In the Hamptons, A Child's Nativity,* and *Among the Alternatives*

POETRY, *The Life Beside This One, The Quiet Life, That Summer, The Companion, For Whiskey, Comparing the Literature, Three, Out of England, The Mirror,* and *For the Children, About Their Deaths*

SHENANDOAH, *At the Restaurant Polár, The Gifts*

Library of Congress catalog card number 75-4086
ISBN 0-689-10669-6
Published simultaneously in Canada by McClelland and Stewart Ltd
Manufactured in the United States of America by
Halliday Lithograph Corporation, West Hanover and Plympton, Massachusetts
Designed by Harry Ford
First Edition

FOR MY WIFE

The hosts of the dead are transformed
And we shall be changed
Into perfect, unmarried strangers.

Then we shall put our imperfections
Into the ground like stones
And be whole and needless.
But now they are ours.
We find ourselves wanting
No end to our incompletion
Or the hard impermanent years
That hasten to their perfection

Where the hosts of the dead are transformed
And we shall be changed
Into perfect and endless strangers.

I THE LIFE BESIDE THIS ONE

II CRUSOE CONTINUING

III FOR MY MOTHER IN THE WOODS

IV RUNNING IT BACKWARD

I *The Life Beside This One*

THE LIFE BESIDE THIS ONE

In the life you lead
Beside this one,
It is natural for you
To resemble America.
You require one woman.
You give her your name.

You work, you love;
You take satisfaction.
You are the president of something.
You are the same.

The children are clean,
They turn into lawyers.
They write long letters
And come home for Christmas.

It is a kind of Connecticut
Not to be twenty-five again.
Carefully in the evening
You do not think
Of the life you lead
Beside this one.

THE QUIET LIFE

Tired of hanging
Around in himself,
He went out
Into other people.

At length familiar and
Occupying a place in their lives
Like the park one cuts through
On the way to work,

He was the sign
Awaiting the painter
That all day for weeks
Does not say *Buy* or *Enter*.

All night he is the tree
That falls and falls
In the famous dark
And philosophical forest.

THE COMPANION

I shall begin
To appear too often.
You will not recall
When first you saw me.

I shall arrive
At the light beside you.
Catching a plane
You will observe me.

I shall never speak.
I will never ignore you.
I shall open a door.
You will pass before me.

I will stand
In a line behind you.
Whatever you do
I shall be the same.

Nobody else
Will ever believe you.
Soon you will find
You are looking for me.

The day will come,
It is getting closer,
When I shall stand
At every corner.

Then you will know
That you deserve me
And there will be
No more excuses.

THE DEPARTURE

Whatever you do
Occurs at a distance.
It is never yours.
You are signing the paper.
You order it done.
It will happen without you.

You are uttering words.
You cannot hear them.
The other people
Are writing them down.
Then they arise.
They are moving toward you.

You are drawing away.
You are leaving the station.
You wave goodbye.
It is your departure.
You are standing here.
You are on your journey.

SENTENCE

It has happened before.
It is bound to happen.
You are nobody else.
It is what you mean.

There is nothing to do.
And you believe that.
You are nobody else.
It will happen again.

THAT SUMMER

Back there in the trivial weather
The girls are seventeen;
The boys loll in their jobs.
It is that summer forever.

And the dead are everywhere
And look forward to supper.
One is gutting a fish.
Another is writing a letter.

But beyond September
Our lives
Wait to begin.
When we arrive

In that perfect, pointless
Summer forever
The dead everywhere
Look forward to supper.

II *Crusoe Continuing*

CRUSOE CONTINUING

Father told me but
I did not believe.
I could not evade
The future beyond Brazil.

In that Eden of obstacles
The tropical eye
Of God shone
On my bread.
Black as Friday
He walked like Father
In my dreams full of advice.
I dived for him
Among my Bibles
Where his word was
Faith. And work.

Obedience and the valuable
Junk of Europe sustained me
To the renovation of my dust.
Eating twenty-eight
Years of my labor,
I am born again,
Four times the phoenix
And a self-made man.

This side of the island,
Home closes like a bank
On my life full of money.
Father is dead. I am
Where I began,
At my destination.

Read me. I am
Your father who labors
And does not mention women.
Imagining America
As work, I invent you.
Set forth
On my further adventures.
Page by page
Approach my end.

AT FOREST LAWN CEMETERY

Out of love with the real,
I am at home here
At the west end of history
In this suburb of death.

To this destination
Beyond satire
All signs have directed me:
To this comfortable marble
Memento mori we
Come to forget ,
Its idea of the past
An unserious decor,
The scrapings of Europe,
The perfect copy.

Here death is Babyland's
Heartshaped acre
Where at Christmas
Above their personal
Identical trees
The desolate, non-sectarian
Incorruptible dead
Christian babies will rise
Singing *O Tannenbaum*
As they dance in their spices.
Beyond the turnstiles
Of the interfaith cathedral,
In "the largest oil
Painting in the world"
And a weather
Impossible for crucifixions,
Christ is forever
Not yet nailed up.

What is left but
(Having mailed Mother
Twelve tiny views
Of Forest Lawn
In a rubberoid nutshell)
To descend at once
Into Los Angeles?
Tomorrow, perhaps,
Disneyland's miles of mild
Rational entertainment;
Or the Homes of the Stars
And the Universal lot.

NEAR THE POTOMAC

A family graveyard in Fairfax County

How shall I think of them,
These deep American
Ancestors of whom I know
Little except that they lived here
Or nearby most of their lives?
Surely most of their lives
Were not more interesting
Or cheerful than mine is?
Except that they lived here
Or nearby, in their destination.

Imagine one, then,
Head full of the high-sounding
Republic, thinking sometimes in Latin,
As one who might live in a book,
Confidently archaic
In dignity like Adam's,
Armed in his manners;

And say to him, *Father,*
Was I your intention,
You who were yourself for years,
Not your habits as I am?
Am I what you mean,
Practicing my vacant skill
Where piece by piece the future
Assembled beyond the horizon
Visible from your hill?

At Arlington the national dead
Muse on their barbered hill.
Downstream, Mt. Vernon's
Clean museum,
Chic in death,
Blazes at the Potomac.

But no ideas
Gather about these graves;
Only now and then
A few of their ignorant children.
Here in these actual weeds
In poetical tangles
Is a family plot
Become a pointless story.

Downhill the Interstate
Searches out Richmond.
Scott's Run
Crawls in a drain,
Toils in the new dark
Toward some conclusion.
Here is a place
No longer.
This is a piece
Of a distance between.
The houses are marching.
Earthmovers, hugely georgic,
Farm the sold field.
We got our million.

IN THE HAMPTONS

Much here is historical
And dull, but not therefore.
What has occurred since
Is the rich.
Here, fully clothed,
They summered relentlessly
Miles from the nearest
Jew or serious painter.
All day their trim,
Pictorial waves
Relaxed ashore
In weather clear as gin.

But the last man in America
To play tennis in flannels
Is dead. Beyond Queens,
Borough of cemeteries,
Dressed in an idea
About taste as money,
A future approaches
The invented lanes;
To these few beautiful,
Talkative miles
Of bad behavior
The repressed returns.

Although all night
At Montauk,
An end of America,
Washington's light
Still solves again
The pointless, eastward water,
Out of the drama of the dark
The snazzy summer theatre takes us in.

III   *For My Mother in the Woods*

FOR MY MOTHER IN THE WOODS

In the story I tell
We are still sitting there
In that story her childhood
That she is unfolding about her
While the surprising
Water falls through the woods
Out of the hill under her mother's garden.

Here we have walked through the woods
Where she walked with her mother,
And the water is falling exactly where they found it,
And I sit on the stone where she sat
Before I was there, before her childhood
Turned into the world where I sit
In her marvellous story.

I am sitting there now
In the story I tell
In the place I shall never revisit,
I with my mother and she
Perhaps with hers;
And the stone is there;
And the water is there as it was,
And still it is going away and is not returning.

ANECDOTES OF FATHERS

I.

Out of the cage
Of his photograph's frame
In the 1893
Georgia yearbook
Glares the collected rage
Of Major Charles Morris, C.S.A.,
A.M., The University of Virginia,
Professor of *Belles Lettres*;
American as the nineteenth century;
Each hair explicit.

Unimaginable! What is it
About Great-grandfather
Besides part of a name,
His profession and anger
That I inherit?

His pen that would
Correct Death
Visibly describes
Nothing in a book.

2.

And you, Grandfather John,
Almost your name,
I have forgotten you
Until you are only
When I am four:
An old man crossing
An unplaceable street.

No doubt you live
Wrong in my recollection
Of the recollections of others:
The only agnostic
Professor of German
In Georgia with a Catholic wife,
Death on Talmadge
And big-time football,
You plagued your puzzled
All-Americans to translate
"I would have been here earlier
Had not the innkeeper's daughter
Tied my horse to a tree."

You wrote about ringmail
In Simplified Spelling.
But you will not translate.
Would I had been here earlier,
Uber die Strasse gehende Mann.

SUBURBAN PASTORALS

For Anne

1. *Not Gardening*

Last year the lilac
Labored for a single bloom
And now—*bonanza*—
A burst of confident
Lavender self-applause!

Ignoring it,
Walking apart, together
We agree
On keeping a silence
We do not understand.
This year we visit
Only the tiny
Quiet careful
Green return.

Day after day we bring
Our perfect
Ignorance to it:
The prayer of the eye
To the gradual leaf.
It is a kind of listening
As to the multitudinous
Descending silent snow.

This is what we are doing:
Hands empty of water or knives,
We are not gardening.
Silence is growing
Under the trees
We cannot name.

2. *Summer School*

The Atlantic, in which
In Missouri I cannot believe,
Calls us like home
To the east where the past
In its vivid jackets
Gathers for cocktails
On remarkable lawns.
There we are known
For our childhood,
Our solemn promise
Passing among the tall
Convivial dead.

This year we choose
To steam in our virtue.
I labor for winter;
I am teaching the past
To paint our walls.
This is the summer school,
To be working for winter,
The good weather
Over our heads.

Gradually in the evening
Under the trees
That are outlasting us,
We disappear. The mothers,
The mothers are calling
The children of others,
Calling them home.
Ice dies in our glasses.
We are keeping our promise.
This is our place
Where we do not belong.

3. *Saving the Daylight*

While the darkness
Assembles about us
Its brilliant toy,
Putting together
Every evening,
That huge machine,

This is what
We are doing
Gathering leaves:
Turning into
Another weather;
Burning summer
In the burning time.

This is a way
Of saving the daylight:
Burning brightness
In the winter time.
This is what
We are doing,
Gathering darkness.

4. House Holding

Years of the Missouri
Woods blaze at our fire
Where we live with our parents'
Decisions about what
Is beautiful and lasts.

This house, this imitation
Of England we did not build,
Excludes the middle
American dark where the neighbors
Walk their own choice in dogs,
Pursuing their private
Preferences into their future.

Upstairs the children are growing.
Though pipes burst
And floods are expected,
We hold the whole
House in our hands. The years,
The years are warming our faces.

IN THE RESTAURANT POLÁR

In Kyoto's rooftop
Restaurant Polár
My table's particular
Fifteen ice inches
Of carved polar bear
Diminish quietly.
He weeps all over
Into the radishes
The size of mice
(Said to be raised
From only the purest garbage)
That he is set to guard.

With what mysterious
Pointless care
This possibly comical
Creature has been made
To disappear!
It is 1955. Under miles
Of wet roofs in all directions
Japan is waiting, as if it were
The future. He is a thing of tears.

BURNING THE HOUSES: A HISTORY

25 West Tenth Street, 1940

Odd to hear him
"Out of the Past"
For Bond bread at 6:30
On WOR,
The Lone Ranger
Who in a business suit
Lived in person
On the first floor.

In our floor-through fifth
With woodburning fireplace,
Luxurious even in 1940
At seventy-five a month,
I sickened obscurely,
Feeling nothing
Among the furniture
That resembled home.

The doctor said I'd grown
Too big for my heart.
So no more school,
Where, after rooftop volleyball,
In the Grace Church
Episcopal dark and smells,
Cornwallis surrendered
In 8 mm. silence,
The band in captions
Energetically not playing
The World Turned Upside Down.

All day at home now,
Glutting on Oz and Kipling,
I did not speak
To our sort-of governess,
An exiled German
Female dentist,
I and my sister
Her unworthy only work.
Marching my Woolworth's
World War I
Infantry while the glue
Dried on my Strombecker
Models of the new
North Carolina and B-17,
I had the whole apartment
For my un-outgrown
Child's Garden of Verses
Land of Counterpane.

While Mussolini too
Invaded France
And the radio
Nominated Willkie,
I carved on my pine chest
From Georgia the Tin Woodman's
Insensate head and hat.
Amnesiac Lorenzo Jones
Strayed from his name
Each day at 4:30,
Lost for months
Inside my Philco.

Those were the days
Among the litter of my skill
At carving scotties out of Oxydol
I liked to burn my cardboard
Carton houses in the fireplace.
I'd hold my breath
Until the flames
Leaned from the windows
Like people out of each intense
Boxful of emptiness.

Tiny to feel that now,
As I gaze in my prose
Way and recollection
At what I do not remember:
The back of a house
On West Eleventh Street.
Wars away it waits
To be suddenly nothing,
A violent absence
That my unborn sister's
Madeira schoolmate,
Raging, alone with others
In their distant reasons,
Burning her lessons,
Will grow up to say.

While the World's Fair
Closes behind the Germans,
Mother will marry.
We will move away
Into Connecticut
Where the war began.

THE RETURNS

You are returning
These nights
In your dark suit
In your fashion.

All night I am nine.
You are never wrong.
I shall never be home in time.
You smile at Mother.

Sometimes you die
Before I answer your letter,
A scrupulous hand
Enclosing money.

Every morning
I am your age
In your dark suit.
It wears like iron.

THE WATERING TROUGH

No drink so cool
As from that spout!

And in the later day
Though warm as blood
In the dark wood,
Water we led the horses to—
Lady and David Gray, Parfait,
Who always drank.

FOR WHISKEY

Not yet usually
In the daytime
But all evening I
Raise my favorite
Color to my face.

On three now the brain
Hooks like a tarpon.
No more the good
Hour when work
Shaped ahead
Like an achievement.

O, always to live
In that amber
Where, *boulevardier,*
The right word
Strolled in the blood;

Never to write
A poem unpleasant
As some thoughts,
Iron ideas,
A life like bone.

FOR THE CHILDREN,
ABOUT THEIR DEATHS

In the beginning of course
May they be far, be waiting
Where you will like to be,
On the other side of your labor.

Look! You are running toward them
Into your work and love
As if to your salvation.
They are why you are not
The beasts who are never changing.
They are why you are moving.

After your marriage and work,
After all you have chosen,
May they belong to you.
Then you are finally yours,
Choosing what you have chosen.

I who will die in my childhood
Where we could see for miles
Am talking about myself.
I write you a letter from there.
You will come to your own conclusions.

IV   *Running It Backward*

RUNNING IT BACKWARD

A simple flick of the switch
And his familiar figure
Steps back out of the doorway,
Out of the fond familiar arms
That now drop eagerly to her sides.
Backward he rapidly walks
On the crazy pavement
Into his car whose door
Flies into his hand at a gesture;
Expertly staring ahead, he
Reverses quickly out of the picture.

At first it is mildly funny
Watching him perform
With such cheerful address
These difficult backward
Easy forward things.
So when the whiskey
Arises into the bottle
And, smiling,
He refuses his first job
And returns the diploma
With a firm handshake,
We laugh.
          But suddenly
It is turning serious, we see
That he is going
Where we do not wish to follow.
That smile still on his face
But growing doubtful now,
He is climbing down
Out of his college,
Through algebra and beginning French
Into a taste for Coca-Cola.

Now quickly he falls
Through the grades
Into his shorts
And the birthday parties.
Though a profusion of gifts
Resume their brilliant paper,
There, as the breath returns
To him who gave it
And laughter fades
To pure expectancy,
Before the match withdraws
That seemed to lean
To seem to put them out,
Out of the dark the candles come
At once alight.

Here with a flick of the switch
It is time to be stopping,
For looking ahead
We foresee what is true
But improper to be shown:
How, soon, he is going faster,
How he lapses from language
Into helpless tears,
A rage beneath naming
Shaking him as he dwindles;
How, behind his silent scream,
He disappears
In a fury of flapping and clicking
Into the dark and shining
Whirring tiny mouth of the machine.

BEGINNING A POEM ABOUT MY DOG

Have I never known any extraordinary
Animals I could write a poem about,
Models, as in poetry they usually are,
Of what we have left behind
In George MacBeth's *Penguin
Book of Animal Verse*—
Their patience, say, and natural grace
And the holy innocence of their rapacity,
For which, naturally, we feel nostalgic?

Yes. I will write about my dog Bosco
Who bites his tail until he is
A dog with a sore tail,
Who swallows his fur like a cat
And is violently anti-Negro.
I shall write about him in a plain flat
Style so that the essential extraordinary
Ordinary *reality* of him will come out
And what a loss it is to us
That we are not like that
Any longer, having invented God
And Motive and the automobile,
Which separates us so from the Natural
And our senses and instincts and like that,
And Consciousness, that curse, that makes us
Want to write poems for the *Penguin
Book of Animal Verse* (edited
By George MacBeth, who is not inhuman)
About what a loss it is to us
That we are not like that.

True, dogs are not really the best
Examples of all that, as I shall note;
Noting too that with them as with ourselves
It is all our fault, though even they
Do not join us in our occasional
Passion for things like inedible justice
Or poems in *The Penguin Book of Animal Verse*.

COMPARING THE LITERATURE

Fresh from his
History of Water
And *The Theory of Halves*,
The professor arrives.
Perhaps he has come
To compare the literature.

He will not begin
With poems, likening them
To fathers or the stones
In brooks for telling
Always the old
Same voluble story.

Diligently he resembles
The Form of the Essay.
He is probably happy
Like the childhood of others.
The sun is making
It perfectly clear.

THREE

Mouth's disfurnished eyes
Distinguish only size.
He often has confessed
The newborn have it best:
Who hangs upon the teat
Has all the world to eat.

When Cock is on his walk
He has no time for talk.
Clenched in his appetites
He trawls the Village nights.
Pacifically he sighs
Between whatever thighs.

And I? My only lusts
This set of thin disgusts,
I find the every other
Is never worth the bother.
My candy on the shelf,
I keep me to myself.

OUT OF ENGLAND

The landscape opened like a children's book.
    The village seemed a toy.
This is the past, he thought. *It has a look*
    Of careful joy.

And is so small. A species of Japan.
    Behind each perfect gate
Cottages made of tourist-poster stone
    Exactly wait.

All is in place. Yet nothing is arranged.
    It's like an accident:
It only happened. But it can't be changed:
    As if it meant.

Say it were so. How could he then withstand,
    As if it hid a harm,
The low, relentless, beautiful command
    Of all that charm?

Home in America he ponders this,
    Where the great rivers drain
Lost clapboard towns, serious villages,
    Miles of vague plain.

THE GIFTS

All year in the appropriate North his elves,
Working like Germans in our pretty tale,
Labor for nothing. Nothing is for sale.
A brilliant junk amasses on the shelves.

Each child is flat in his exhausted bed.
As a cold breath upon the million fires
Out of the year huge Santa Claus transpires
To leave each granted wish behind for dead.

They are the day when nothing is for sale
And at great cost. Though trivial defects
At once appear, at first no one suspects
Each lovely whole shebang's designed to fail.

KILLING THE CHILDREN

"I told her it was the dogs barking."
Myra Hindley, the Moors murderess

We all grow used to our lives.
They are like a book I am reading.
At night I lay it aside.
I take it up in the morning.

Here we are killing the children.
It is like a train I am riding.
This is a book I am reading.
Those are dogs that are barking.

I can never do anything wrong.
It is dull in the book I am reading.
Nothing happens to me.
That is why it is normal.

I lay it aside like a book.
Here is our destination.
We all grow used to our lives.
In the end it feels like wisdom.

LOOKING FOR IT

Getting away, leaving
Yourself behind you,
Arrive at the motel
Idea of comfort.
Unpack your careful
Suit, the books
Foreseen for the odd
Appetites of isolation,
The bottle provided
Against a dry state.
At last you are nowhere,
The television arguing
A strange local news.

Look for it first
Among the shirts—
Your speech, the letter.
Suddenly over
And over it is not
There nor in the last
Improbable pocket.
It is nowhere,
What you must always
Remember not to forget,
Getting away, leaving
Yourself behind you
Like debt, like satisfaction.

GOING BACK FOR THE TWENTIETH

The dead and the poor of course
Do not return. Only the not unsuccessful
Show up with our smiles
And polite, irrelevant wives
Here the age of our mothers.
Nicknames spring
To our lips like wit.

But whatever we do
We do not impress us,
Having known us when.
All day in the marvellous view
Under our funny hats
Over and over again
We say we have hardly changed.
Today it seems to be true.

Tomorrow after the files
Of the young have marched among us,
Beginning and festive in their final black,
It will be time to drive
Away from the marvellous view,
Time to be going back
Home again to our lives.
The children wait for our wives.
Taking away our smiles
Under our funny hats
The years turn over like miles.

FOR THE MAN IN THE MIRROR

Over my shoulder we part,
I to my sleep
And usual usual dreams
And he—to what?
Into what eight-hour future
He carries our worried face
I can only suppose.
He is drawing away,
He is turning into the darkness
Behind the backward door.

Perhaps in his wish
He disappears
Into another country
Under a colder sky.
There the corrected stars
In the chime of their causes
Turn in a perfect journey.

But I hope he is only
Doing my sleep
And that is his duty:
To turn as I turn
In the slow world
And always do it exactly.
I hope he is drawing my breath
Into his darkness
And that is his work.
May he continue.

Whatever he does,
May he arrive in the morning
Exactly on time
Imperceptibly older.
We lean to our knives
In the dance we are leading.
We are holding our breath
In the long world. May we continue.

A CHILD'S NATIVITY

Struck dumb at arm's length,
The crayon Madonna regards
As if with aversion
Her terrific baby,
A three-foot man
She holds only in her hands.
He stares like guns.

Angels are falling
Under a sharp star,
Alleluias
Issue from their heads.
Enormous thin sheep
Intent as wolves
Surround Him.

OWNING YOUR OWN HOME

Perhaps for the children
This will be where
Everything happens.
Alice will disappear
Into your mirror
And book after book
Of ladies withdraw
Into what you never call
The withdrawing room or parlor;
Your every room upstairs
Full of the long diseases
The fictional old
Are dying of,
Deep in their books
A stream of heroes
Issue from your door.

But the loud books you read
Will never contrive
To happen here.
Your murders occur
In permanent
Rooms elsewhere.
For you it is other houses
That are everywhere.

Still, gradually even you
Will find the stair
Descends to the right place
And wherever you set
Foot is an answering floor.
At last, familiar,
It will turn into the strange
Known houses of dreams
Where a forgotten room
Discovers work like Bluebeard's
Behind a sudden door.

Slowly the old
Terrors arrive
Like forwarded mail;
Assemble like an inheritance,
A deep furniture
That knows you,
In the new hall.

Here are the words
You heard behind the sofa.
Here is the old cellar.
Here is the attic floor.
Now beyond all the owing
And the last payment
You have your house
Where nothing changes.
It is like your life.
Now it is always.
Finally it is yours.

THE CURE

The intellectual life over at last
And the children no longer a worry,
He will not despond any more,
Will not be one of the dolorists
Who have their pain and love it,
It being theirs, and go home to it,
Where it understands what they are,
And carry it to the doctor
Who will make it whole and well.

Now he is ready for the pleasant pleasures.
There is no need to wish to be happy again.
At last the years resemble one another.
Avanti! Avanti! Here is the center of all!

FOR DEAD HORSES

Hell is perhaps
Cambridge or some
Other witticism where
The interesting live
Among their interests
And agree entirely except.

How our fond hearts
Beat under their fat
When the single wills
Who do not love us
Gather unanimous
In electric colors!

Our desires assemble
Outside their music;
But this and that
Will not permit.
Life is at home
Among the children
Who do not hate us yet.

LOOKING AT ANIMALS

Under the hill where the museum
Pretends to be Europe,
A huge statuary
Weathering on its walls,
Prowling the zoo
I look for my entertainment
For something to do.

Safe as sheep in their harmless ditches and houses
They are beautiful here
In the kind garden of containment.
It is the zoological condition. Their pastors arrive
In green on time on their electric carts.
All of the animals seem to thrive
On their diet of parts.
They are looking well for my entertainment.

Still, though the walrus, popular and immense
In his pool and pet name,
Seems to want nothing
But applause and fish,
The spectacle bear keeps missing
The peanuts I throw,
As if he had learned about trying.
Only the serpents untying
Themselves like lively rope
Seem to cover their rock
In their dangerous nature.
The purposive merciless lion
Drills his obsession
For hours through its paces;
He punishes, he hurts
It to the edge of exhaustion.

It is the zoological condition.
Hugely the great apes
In another dimension
Do nothing together,
Alone in concert.
I stare till they are dull
Types of a shape.
I raise my eyes up to the hill.
Our images stare
Down from the stone walls
Like men and are no help

JACOB

All summer this appetite grew
And in November we killed him.

But not for him the sudden,
Head-down, squealing,
Terrific truss-up
And his heart to help
Clean him of his life.
Because 1 gave him a name,
Having arranged the garbage
Into five valuable feet
Or so of the huge pounds
Of his sort of animal,
He died kindly of a gun.

All winter the pale
Pink taint of his blood
Came to the table.
Because I had said who he was
He would never be clean of his life.
I offer you in his name
The color and price of mercy.

AMONG THE ALTERNATIVES

At the expensive summer
Island dump
Hundreds of gulls prove
Loudly almost nothing
That we refuse
But tin and glass is inedible.
Over their noise
My boy at four is
Delighted with this
Sprightly, cacophonous
Country of garbage,
This deep acre, this ditch
Full of the lush trash of the rich.

Afterward, up the road,
We pause in a low wood
Where, in perfect silence,
Other leftovers
Hugely collect.
Wreck piled on wreck,
All color and size,
Darts, Ramblers and Rovers
Invisibly oxidize,
Go nowhere slowly
In their hundreds.
This is the garden of motion.
We love this beautiful *dreck*.

At four my son believes
They drive here to die.
Neither do I reflect
On these still stacks
As violence.
What moves us is
The abundance of this
Resistance, this
Near-stasis.

Gulls are the garbage
Way of surviving.
Under these vegetable trees
Is nothing to burn or eat.
I think we think
These tons the shape
Of teleology
Under arrest
Heroic as work.
What lasts is waste.

AGAINST SILENCE

Everywhere men
Are dying always
In their own tongue
Where I could not
Order dinner,
Every last
Word they utter
A last word
Momentarily;
Composing themselves:
The unmeditated
Exact tenses
They temporarily
Are finally;

And every last
Perhaps nonsensical
Death sentence
A resurrection:
Hankering forward
Against silence,
Building, building;
Articulate
As a snake's back,
As finely moving
Toward silence,
Its perfection;
Finishing something;
Building unbuilding.

GREAT WEALTH

It will never die.
It is the grass
In the image of kings.

I desire it
As if it were wisdom.
There I am writing
Pages full of contentment.
It is like an evening
Where I have never been.

It is what
Spinoza believes in.
If you are rich
Put forth your hand.
It is the simple thing.

ALWAYS WALKING

Sometimes you are
Always walking.
The lane is turning.
Sometimes you are
Coming to that place.

Ah, the good place!
And they are waiting
For you, the others,
The others who know you
And still they love you.

The lane is turning.
You are always walking.
Sometimes you are
A whole life
Coming to that place.

THE FATHERS

When we shall finally be
The children's simple story,
The story they tell the children,
Then we shall be the fathers

Dead in their terrible clothes
There on the mantel beside us
Looking out of their eyes
With their eyes, looking before us.

THE LOCKED COAST

In this weather
As an excuse
Book after book
Goes unwritten.

At night I am
A man in China.
I get up
The color of gold.

Where have I been?
The wind is rising.
Tomorrow will come.
It is all beginning.

The ship sails
In Caesar's eye.
The prevenient wind
Opens a way.

THANKSGIVING

In childhood you think
This will go on forever.
Your elders are talking.
You do not understand.

They are eating pounds
Of the light and the dark.
The bottle is moving.
It passes from hand to hand.
It leans to every glass.
This will go on forever.
The hour will never pass.

At the end of the wine,
Leaving the others talking,
One by one they slip away
To their invisible beds.

Now you are alone.
The bones are clean.
The bottle is empty.
You take the last sip
They leave in every glass.
This meal will never end.

THE MIRROR

Here is a child who is leaning over a paper,
A pencil in hand. And what he seems to be doing
Is drawing or thinking to draw. Or perhaps he is writing,
Writing or drawing a summer he stands by the sea.
He is drawing or writing a child leaning over a paper
Who is perfectly through with the summer, through with the sea.

And that is the world. The world is what he is writing
Or drawing perhaps. The world is the drawing or writing,
Perhaps is the child, perhaps the summer and sea.

JOHN N. MORRIS

John N. Morris was educated at the Augusta Military Academy, Hamilton College, and Columbia University. At present he teaches eighteenth-century English literature at Washington University in St. Louis. He is the author of a critical study, VERSIONS OF THE SELF: STUDIES IN ENGLISH AUTOBIOGRAPHY (1966), *and of an earlier book of poems,* GREEN BUSINESS (1970).